U.S.A. TRAVEL GUIDES

NORTH DAKOTA

BY ANN HEINRICHS • ILLUSTRATED BY MATT KANIA

The Child's World®
childsworld.com

Published by The Child's World®
1980 Lookout Drive • Mankato, MN 56003-1705
800-599-READ • www.childsworld.com

Photo Credits
Photographs ©: Malgorzata Litkowska/Shutterstock
Images, cover, 1; Zack Frank/Shutterstock Images,
7; iStockphoto, 8, 28, 32, 37 (bottom); Drew Tarvin
CC2.0, 11; Andre Jenny Stock Connection Worldwide/
Newscom, 12; Will Kincaid/The Bismarck Tribune/
AP Image, 15; Shutterstock Images, 16, 37 (top); Jerry
Hopman/iStockphoto, 19; a200/a77Wells CC2.0, 20;
Charles Zangle CC2.0, 23; Conny Sjostrom/Shutterstock
Images, 24; Robert Ford/iStockphoto, 27; North Dakota
Department of Transportation, 31; Roderick Eime CC2.0,
35

ISBN 9781503819740
LCCN 2016961187

Printing
Printed in the United States of America
PA02334

Ann Heinrichs is the author of more than 100 books for children and young adults. She has also enjoyed successful careers as a children's book editor and an advertising copywriter. Ann grew up in Fort Smith, Arkansas, and lives in Chicago, Illinois.

post card

About the Author
Ann Heinrichs

Matt Kania loves maps and, as a kid, dreamed of making them. In school he studied geography and cartography, and today he makes maps for a living. Matt's favorite thing about drawing maps is learning about the places they represent. Many of the maps he has created can be found in books, magazines, videos, Web sites, and public places.

post card

About the
Map Illustrator
Matt Kania

On the cover: Bison roam Theodore Roosevelt National Park.

OUR NORTH DAKOTA TRIP

NORTH DAKOTA

Are you ready to tour North Dakota? Just follow that loopy dotted line. Or skip around and make your own tour. Either way, you're in for a great adventure.

You'll hang out with **pioneers**. You'll try on a buffalo robe. You'll learn how explorers lived in the wilderness. You'll see how a power plant creates electricity. You'll meet dinosaurs and prairie dogs.

Does that sound like your kind of fun? Then buckle up and hang on tight. It's time to hit the road!

North Dakota's Nicknames: The Flickertail State and the Peace Garden State

As you travel through North Dakota, watch for all the interesting facts along the way.

CANADA

Dunseith

Minot

Devils Lake

Grand Forks

MINNESOTA

Watford City

Missouri River

Lake Sakakawea

Riverdale

Washburn

NORTH DAKOTA

Carrington

Red River

Badlands

Beulah

West Fargo

Bismarck

94

Jamestown

Medora

Dickinson

Fort Ransom

29

SOUTH DAKOTA

North Dakota is named after the Dakota or Lakota. That means "friends" or "allies."

A point near Rugby is called North America's geographic center. It's the center of the continent when measured from north to south and from east to west.

Wow! A pretty famous president enjoyed the Badlands! Theodore Roosevelt spent time here. He said this helped him become president.

CANADA

Highest Temperature: Steele July 6, 1936 121°F (49°C)

Turtle Mountains

Bottineau

The Turtle Mountains rise in northern North Dakota near Bottineau.

Rugby

Missouri River

Parshall

Devils Lake

Devils Lake

Red River

MINNESOTA

Little Missouri River

Badlands

Theodore Roosevelt National Park

Medora

Steele

Lowest Temperature: Parshall February 15, 1936 −60°F (−51°C)

White Butte

Theodore Roosevelt National Park is named after the 26th president. He had two ranches in this area in the 1880s.

Devils Lake is near the town of Devils Lake. It's North Dakota's largest natural lake. No rivers flow into or out of the lake. Its water is salty.

HIGHEST AND LOWEST POINTS
HIGHEST: White Butte at 3,506 feet (1,069 m)
LOWEST: Red River at 750 feet (229 m)

SOUTH DAKOTA

PAINTED CANYON IN THE BADLANDS

Painted Canyon will take your breath away! Just gaze at its rugged hills and rocks. They're striped in purple, green, yellow, and red.

Painted Canyon is near Medora in the Badlands. It is part of Theodore Roosevelt National Park. The Badlands run alongside the Little Missouri River. Their colorful rocks are worn into strange shapes.

North Dakota also has a big Missouri River. It winds through central and western North Dakota. The Red River is big, too. It forms the state's eastern border.

Fertile farmland covers much of North Dakota. In some areas, the land is almost flat. Other areas have gently rolling hills.

Do you like to hike? Head to the Badlands in Theodore Roosevelt National Park.

SULLYS HILL NATIONAL GAME PRESERVE

You'll love exploring Sullys Hill National Game Preserve. It's on the south shore of Devils Lake. You'll see herds of buffalo, or bison. You'll also spot some elk. They're a really big type of deer.

Lots of prairie dogs live here, too. They dig tunnels to make prairie dog towns. How did they get their name? Because they bark when danger is near!

North Dakota is home to lots of other wildlife, too. Moose live in the Turtle Mountains. Deer and antelopes graze across the plains. Smaller animals scurry through the woodlands and meadows. They include beavers, foxes, rabbits, raccoons, and skunks.

These prairie dogs call North Dakota home.

STATE FLOWER
WILD PRAIRIE ROSE

STATE TREE
AMERICAN ELM

STATE BIRD
WESTERN MEADOWLARK

Chill out, Sparky! That's not a dog barking. It's only a prairie dog.

CANADA

Turtle Mountains

Devils Lake

MINNESOTA

Elk shed their antlers in late winter. The antlers begin growing back in the spring. By fall, they're fully grown.

North Dakota is home to flickertail squirrels. They're a type of ground squirrel. North Dakota is sometimes called the Flickertail State.

SOUTH DAKOTA

The National Park Service has five sites in North Dakota.

North Dakota is one of the top states in number of protected wildlife areas.

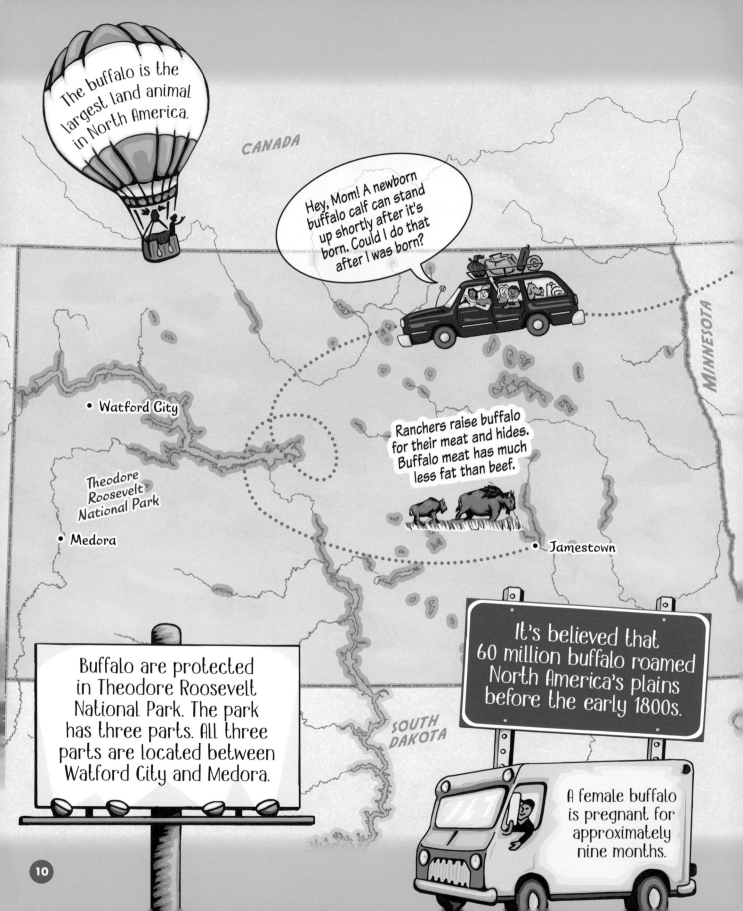

THE BUFFALO OF JAMESTOWN

Buffalo are sometimes hard to spot. But you won't miss the one in Jamestown. It's taller than a two-story building! It's the World's Largest Buffalo. This one is made of concrete. Still, it's mighty scary looking!

Nearby is the National Buffalo Museum. Real buffalo roam the surrounding hills. One was named White Cloud. She was famous. But she died in November 2016. She was a rare white buffalo. White Cloud was sacred to many Native American groups.

Millions of buffalo once grazed across the plains. But hunters pretty much wiped them out. Very few are left now. North Dakota has several protected buffalo herds. Many private ranches raise buffalo, too.

The buffalo statue towers at 26 feet (8 m) tall. He even has a name: Dakota Thunder!

A big *Triceratops* skull guards the entrance. Are you brave enough to go in? You'll be glad you did. This is Dickinson Museum Center's Dinosaur Museum!

The Dinosaur Museum displays real dinosaur bones. Some of the bones are from an *Edmontosaurus*. It was discovered by the museum's curator and his father in 2009. They found the bones in Montana. Visit the museum to learn more about the dinosaur's history.

The Dickinson Museum Center is made up of multiple museums. Others include an art museum and one on the agricultural history of the area.

Some buildings in the Dickinson Museum Center celebrate different heritages, such as the Czech Town Hall.

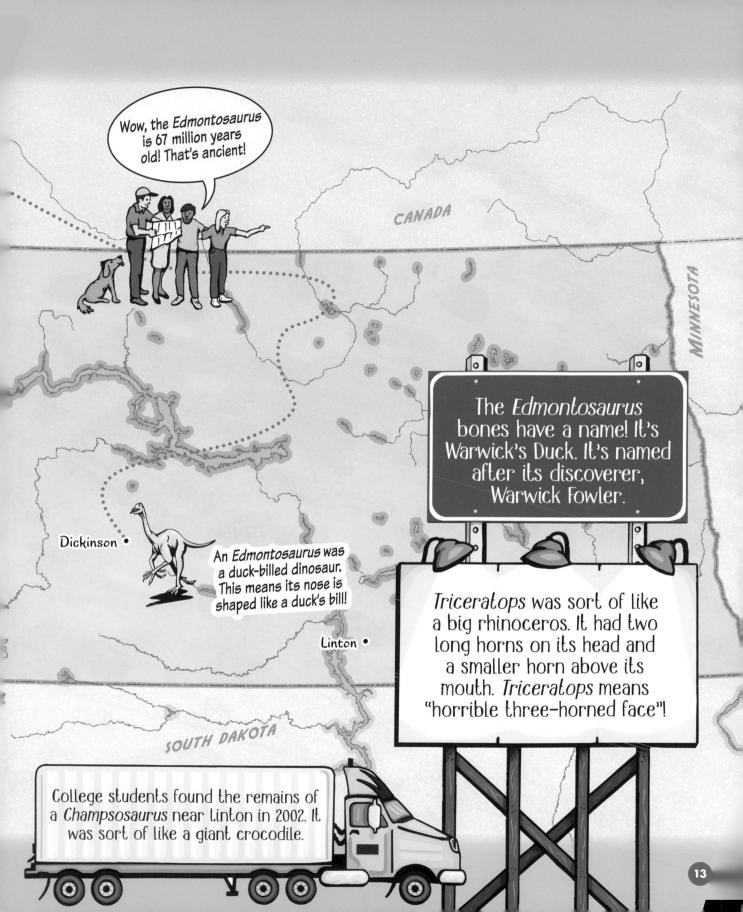

Cool! They even have dance contests for little kids!

CANADA

Who Lived Here before Europeans Arrived? Arikara, Chippewa, Hidatsa, Lakota, Mandan, and Assiniboine

MINNESOTA

Stanton •

★ Bismarck

The United Tribes of North Dakota include the Spirit Lake Nation, the Sisseton-Wahpeton, the Standing Rock Sioux, the Turtle Mountain Band of Chippewa, and the Three Affiliated Tribes of Fort Berthold (Arikara, Hidatsa, and Mandan).

SOUTH DAKOTA

Knife River Indian Villages National Historic Site is near Stanton. It preserves the remains of five Hidatsa and Mandan villages.

The Lakota were North Dakota's largest Native American group when white people first arrived.

THE UNITED TRIBES INTERNATIONAL POWWOW IN BISMARCK

Watch the dancers in spectacular costumes. Hear the deep throb of the drums. It's the United Tribes Technical College **International** Powwow!

This is one of the nation's biggest Native American festivals. More than 70 Native American groups attend. They take part in dance and drumming contests. And they offer **traditional** foods and crafts.

Native Americans have lived in North Dakota for thousands of years. The Three Affiliated Tribes have lived in earthen lodges. The Spirit Lake Nation once built tepees covered with animal skins. Many of the tribes have hunted buffalo across the plains. The animals provided meat and hides. Even the bones were useful. They were made into tools. Today, many Native Americans still call North Dakota home.

The first United Tribes Technical College International Powwow was held in 1969.

POTATO BOWL USA

Do you like foods such as french fries and baked potatoes? If you do, you'll love Potato Bowl USA in Grand Forks. Just gobble away at the World's Largest French Fry Feed. Do you have any room left in your belly? Don't worry, the festival lasts a week!

Farming is a big **industry** in North Dakota. Farms and ranches cover most of the state. Most farmers grow crops. But many raise beef or dairy cattle.

Wheat is North Dakota's major crop. Fields of golden wheat ripple across the plains. Most of the country's durum wheat grows there.

Get your fill of french fries at Potato Bowl USA in Grand Forks! The festival also celebrates football.

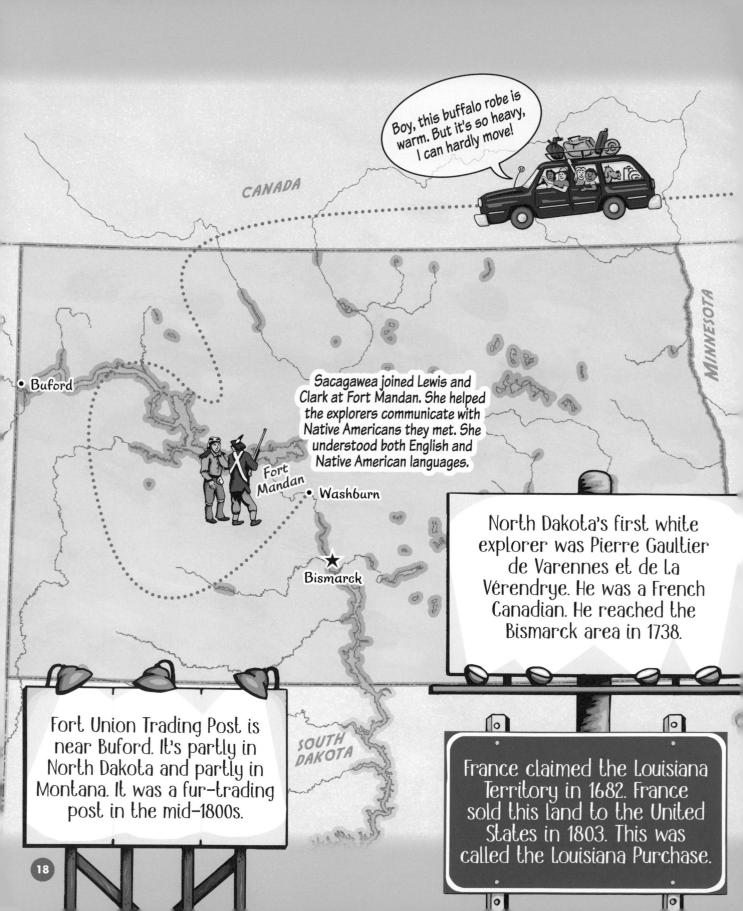

Boy, this buffalo robe is warm. But it's so heavy, I can hardly move!

CANADA

MINNESOTA

• Buford

Sacagawea joined Lewis and Clark at Fort Mandan. She helped the explorers communicate with Native Americans they met. She understood both English and Native American languages.

Fort Mandan

• Washburn

North Dakota's first white explorer was Pierre Gaultier de Varennes et de La Vérendrye. He was a French Canadian. He reached the Bismarck area in 1738.

★ Bismarck

SOUTH DAKOTA

Fort Union Trading Post is near Buford. It's partly in North Dakota and partly in Montana. It was a fur-trading post in the mid-1800s.

France claimed the Louisiana Territory in 1682. France sold this land to the United States in 1803. This was called the Louisiana Purchase.

LEWIS AND CLARK AT FORT MANDAN

Hear about the story of how fur was traded in North Dakota. Learn about the items early explorers would have used on their expedition. You're exploring the Lewis and Clark Interpretive Center in Washburn!

Next, visit nearby Fort Mandan. Explorers built a camp here in 1804. They were Meriwether Lewis and William Clark. Local Mandan people helped them survive the winter.

The United States gained this territory in 1803. President Thomas Jefferson sent Lewis and Clark to explore it. Jefferson wanted them to reach the Pacific Ocean. And they did! They passed through North Dakota again in 1806.

Learn all about the Mandan people who helped Lewis and Clark on their journey when you visit Fort Mandan.

WEST FARGO'S BONANZAVILLE USA

How did North Dakota's pioneers live? Just visit Bonanzaville USA in West Fargo during Pioneer Days. Costumed folks show you how pioneers worked. They're making all they need by hand!

Railroads reached North Dakota in 1872. Then people could travel there easily. Big wheat farms opened in the Red River Valley. They were called **bonanza farms**. Then thousands more settlers began pouring in.

Then gold was discovered in the Dakota Territory in 1874. White settlers were taking over Native Americans' land. Lakota chief Sitting Bull defended his people's land. He led many battles against the U.S. Army. Sitting Bull was forced to surrender in 1881. He was later killed by U.S. troops.

Tour a pioneer schoolhouse at Bonanzaville USA.

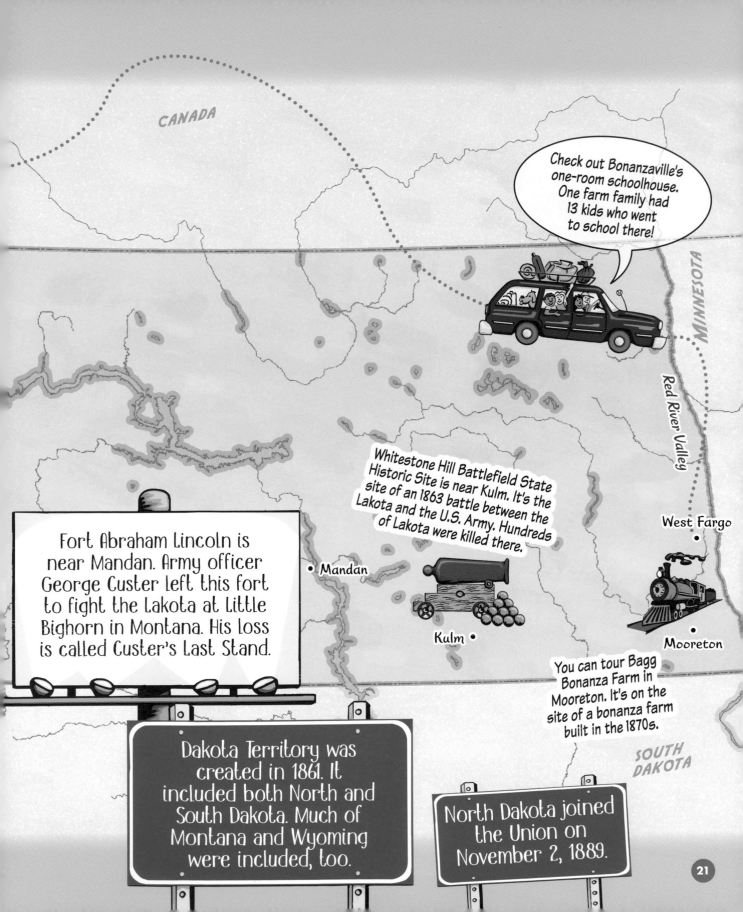

CANADA

MINNESOTA

Check out Bonanzaville's one-room schoolhouse. One farm family had 13 kids who went to school there!

Red River Valley

Whitestone Hill Battlefield State Historic Site is near Kulm. It's the site of an 1863 battle between the Lakota and the U.S. Army. Hundreds of Lakota were killed there.

West Fargo

Fort Abraham Lincoln is near Mandan. Army officer George Custer left this fort to fight the Lakota at Little Bighorn in Montana. His loss is called Custer's Last Stand.

• Mandan

Kulm •

Mooreton

You can tour Bagg Bonanza Farm in Mooreton. It's on the site of a bonanza farm built in the 1870s.

SOUTH DAKOTA

Dakota Territory was created in 1861. It included both North and South Dakota. Much of Montana and Wyoming were included, too.

North Dakota joined the Union on November 2, 1889.

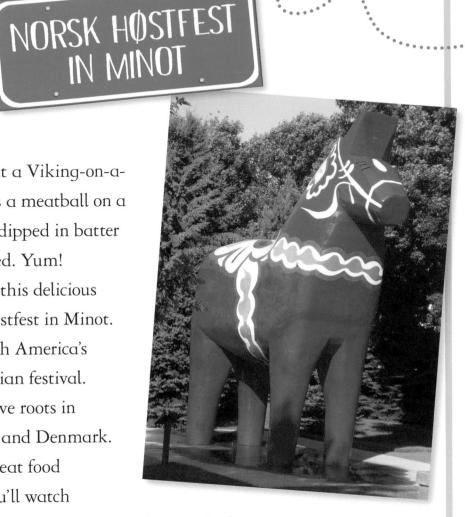

Want to eat a Viking-on-a-stick? It's a meatball on a popsicle stick. It's dipped in batter and then deep-fried. Yum!

You'll sample this delicious treat at Norsk Høstfest in Minot. This event is North America's largest Scandinavian festival. Scandinavians have roots in Norway, Sweden, and Denmark. You'll eat some great food at the festival. You'll watch Scandinavian dancers and craftspeople, too. And you can even dance with a **troll**!

Thousands of settlers began arriving in the 1870s. They included lots of **immigrants**. Many came from Scandinavian countries. Others came from Germany, Russia, and Canada. They all worked hard to build new lives.

Be sure to visit the giant Dalecarlian, a Swedish icon, during Norsk Høstfest!

SODBUSTER DAYS IN FORT RANSOM

What was farming like in the old days? Just check out the Sodbuster Days festival in Fort Ransom. You'll see farmers grinding corn and sawing wood. Others are plowing fields and gathering crops. Horses and mules are pulling their equipment.

Farming is much easier now. Farmers use modern farm machinery. And much of it is made in North Dakota. Factories there make tractors and other farm equipment.

Many foods are cultivated in a factory. Some food plants make flour, pasta, or bread. Others prepare milk or make cheese. All these foods start out as farm products.

How did people farm without modern machinery? Find out at Sodbuster Days!

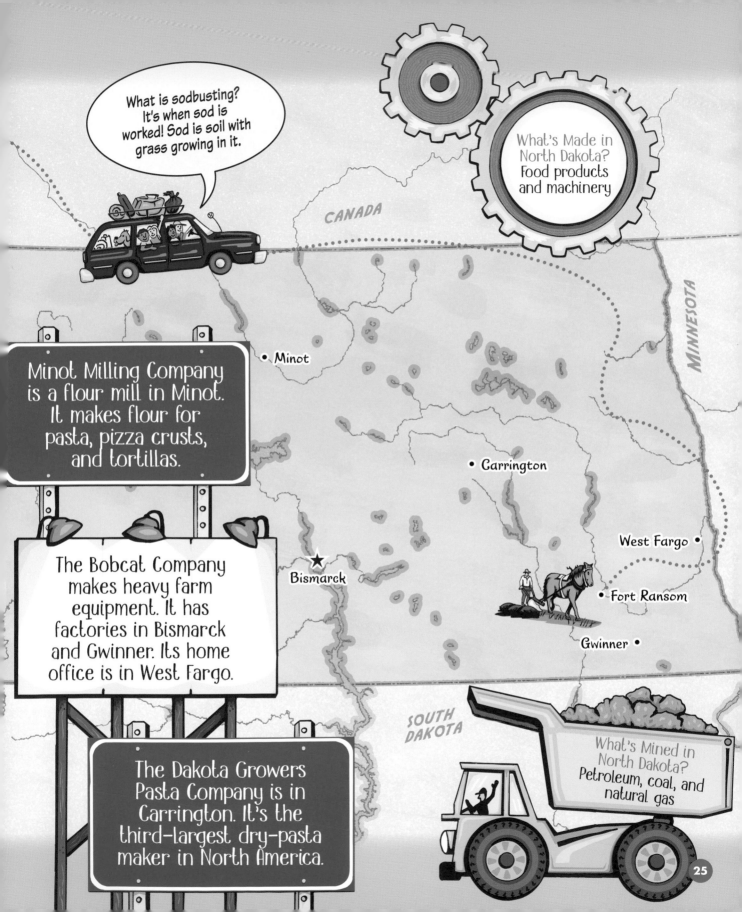

What is sodbusting? It's when sod is worked! Sod is soil with grass growing in it.

What's Made in North Dakota? Food products and machinery

Minot Milling Company is a flour mill in Minot. It makes flour for pasta, pizza crusts, and tortillas.

The Bobcat Company makes heavy farm equipment. It has factories in Bismarck and Gwinner. Its home office is in West Fargo.

The Dakota Growers Pasta Company is in Carrington. It's the third-largest dry-pasta maker in North America.

CANADA

MINNESOTA

• Minot

• Carrington

West Fargo •

★ Bismarck

• Fort Ransom

Gwinner •

SOUTH DAKOTA

What's Mined in North Dakota? Petroleum, coal, and natural gas

25

The North Dakota Mill and Elevator is on the National Register of Historic Places.

North Dakota's first public library opened in Grafton in 1897.

CANADA

Grafton

MINNESOTA

Grand Forks

Wow! They make so many kinds of flour here! Whole wheat flour, pasta flour, pizza flour . . . yum!

The state-owned Bank of North Dakota opened in 1919. This bank made it easier for farmers to borrow money.

SOUTH DAKOTA

The Nonpartisan League was formed in 1915. Its members pushed for laws to help farmers.

Flour contains a substance called gluten. Gluten is what makes bread dough strong and stretchy.

Huge trucks drive in and out. The smokestack belches away. This enormous building is really busy! You'd never guess it's a historic site.

This is the North Dakota Mill and Elevator in Grand Forks. It opened in 1922. And it's still working hard today. Its tall elevators store grain. Its mills grind wheat into flour.

North Dakota farmers were angry in the early 1900s. Big companies owned the grain-processing plants. They made lots of money. But the farmers made very little profit. They demanded help from the state. Soon the state-owned North Dakota Mill opened. It gave farmers good prices for their grain.

The flour from the North Dakota Mill and Elevator can make yummy food, such as pancakes!

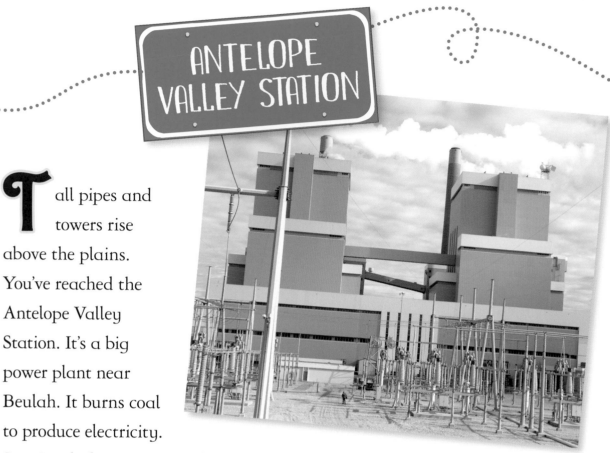

ANTELOPE VALLEY STATION

Tall pipes and towers rise above the plains. You've reached the Antelope Valley Station. It's a big power plant near Beulah. It burns coal to produce electricity. Step inside for a tour. You'll see its massive machines at work.

This power plant burns lignite coal. This type of coal is low in sulfur. When sulfur is burned, it produces sulfur dioxide. This substance causes air pollution.

North Dakota repairs land damaged by mining. The power plants help to protect the **environment**, too. The Antelope Valley Station cleans the gases it releases. Also, it doesn't release unclean water.

Interested in touring a power plant? Check out the Antelope Valley Station.

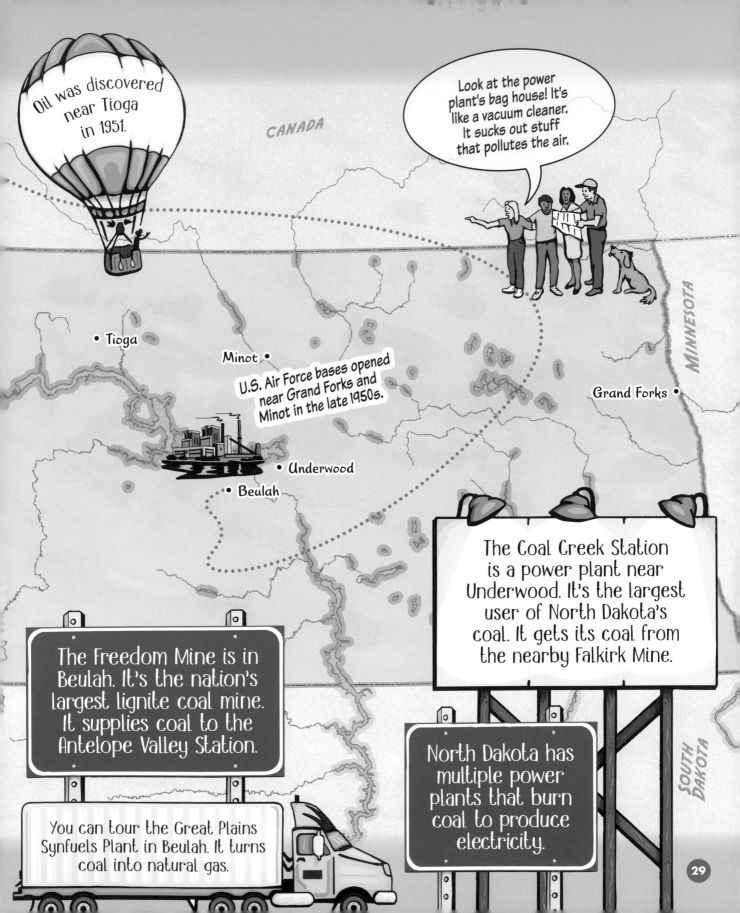

Oil was discovered near Tioga in 1951.

Look at the power plant's bag house! It's like a vacuum cleaner. It sucks out stuff that pollutes the air.

CANADA

MINNESOTA

• Tioga

Minot •

U.S. Air Force bases opened near Grand Forks and Minot in the late 1950s.

Grand Forks •

• Underwood

• Beulah

The Coal Creek Station is a power plant near Underwood. It's the largest user of North Dakota's coal. It gets its coal from the nearby Falkirk Mine.

The Freedom Mine is in Beulah. It's the nation's largest lignite coal mine. It supplies coal to the Antelope Valley Station.

North Dakota has multiple power plants that burn coal to produce electricity.

You can tour the Great Plains Synfuels Plant in Beulah. It turns coal into natural gas.

SOUTH DAKOTA

29

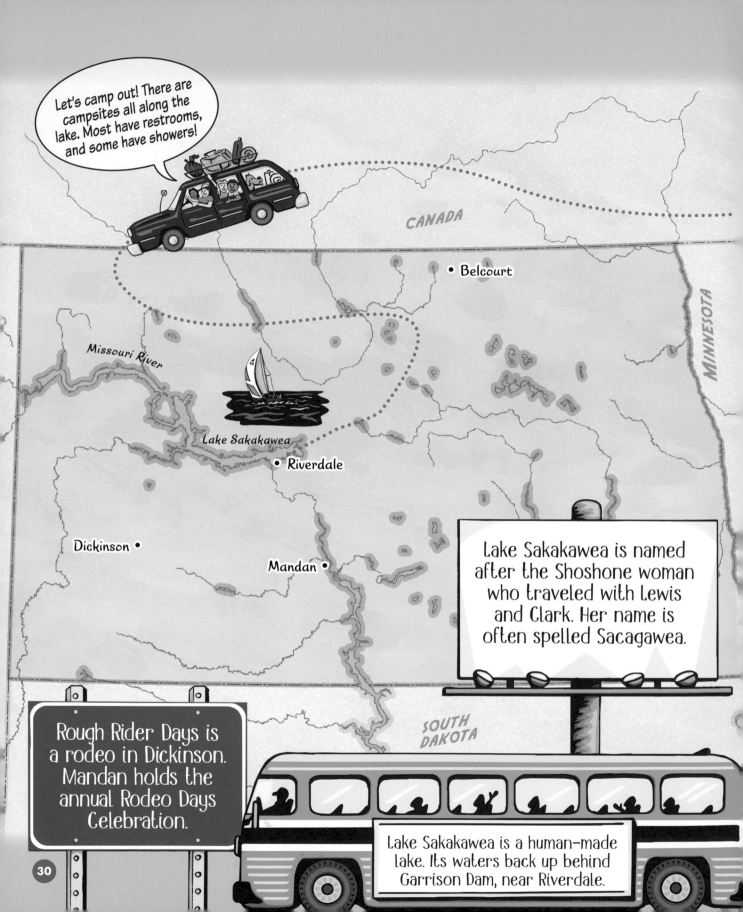

Let's camp out! There are campsites all along the lake. Most have restrooms, and some have showers!

CANADA

MINNESOTA

• Belcourt

Missouri River

Lake Sakakawea

• Riverdale

Dickinson •

Mandan •

Lake Sakakawea is named after the Shoshone woman who traveled with Lewis and Clark. Her name is often spelled Sacagawea.

Rough Rider Days is a rodeo in Dickinson. Mandan holds the annual Rodeo Days Celebration.

SOUTH DAKOTA

Lake Sakakawea is a human-made lake. Its waters back up behind Garrison Dam, near Riverdale.

FUN AT LAKE SAKAKAWEA

Hop in a boat and go fishing. Or maybe you'd like sailboating or windsurfing. There's plenty to do at Lake Sakakawea!

This lake is really long. It stretches for 180 miles (290 km). Its east end is near Riverdale. Its west end is near the Montana border!

North Dakotans enjoy the outdoors. Some people head for the lakes and streams. Others like hiking through wildlife areas. Winter's great for ice-skating, sleigh riding, and skiing. Rodeos are popular events in North Dakota. So are Native American ceremonies such as KeplinFest in Belcourt. It celebrates the Métis and Michif tribes. Many historic sites hold pioneer festivals. And there are farm fairs throughout the state. North Dakota has something for everyone!

The Missouri River runs into Lake Sakakawea. There's much to do here!

THE STATE CAPITOL IN BISMARCK

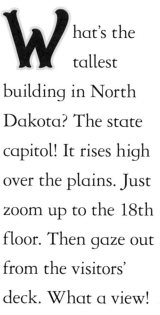

What's the tallest building in North Dakota? The state capitol! It rises high over the plains. Just zoom up to the 18th floor. Then gaze out from the visitors' deck. What a view!

The capitol is North Dakota's state government building. The state government is divided into three branches. Each branch keeps a check on the others. One branch makes state laws. Its members belong to the Legislative Assembly. The governor heads another branch. This branch makes sure laws are obeyed. Judges make up the third branch. They study the laws. Then they decide whether laws have been broken.

Is it a skyscraper or a government building? Both! Head to Bismarck and see for yourself!

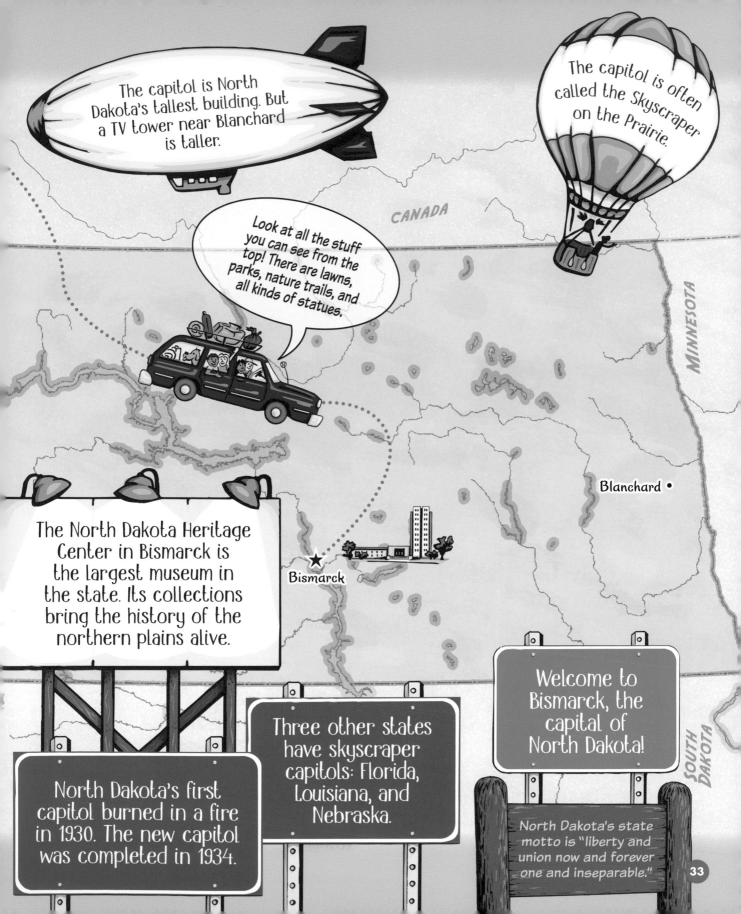

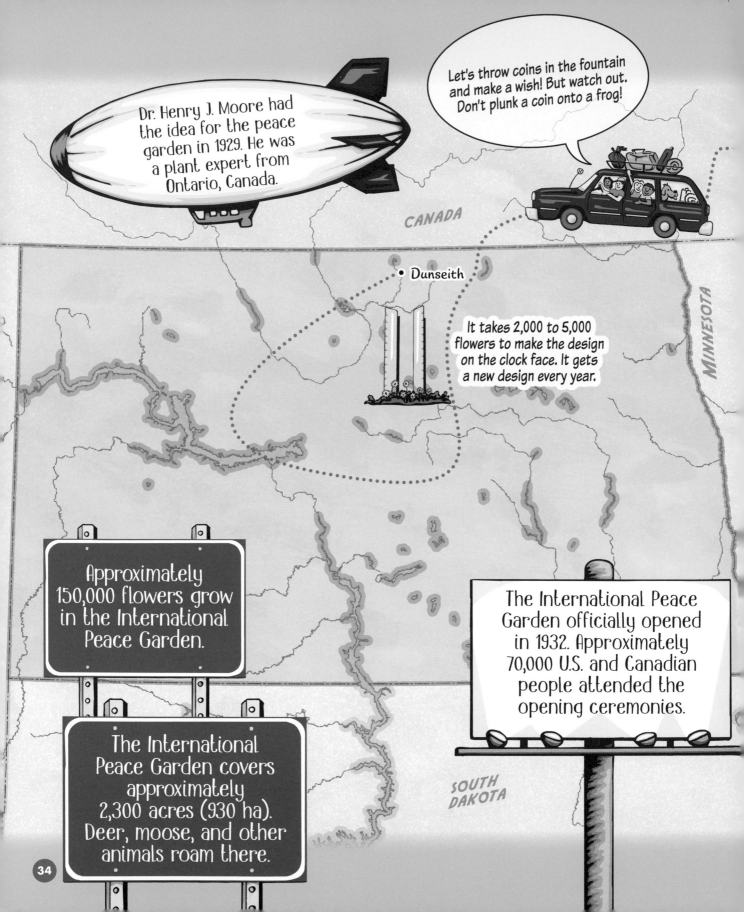

THE INTERNATIONAL PEACE GARDEN

North Dakota is called the Peace Garden State. Why? Because of its International Peace Garden. This beautiful park is north of Dunseith. It's partly in North Dakota and partly in Canada. Canada and the United States built it together. It represents the friendship between the two countries.

Two garden areas are planted in flag designs. They look like the U.S. and Canadian flags. The floral clock is awesome. It's a working clock with flowers for a face.

Japan donated several tall poles to the garden. They say "May Peace Prevail" in 28 languages. What a great message!

Want to take a scenic stroll? Be sure to tour the International Peace Garden.

We visited many amazing places on our trip! We also met a lot of interesting people along the way. Look at the map below. Use your finger to trace all the places we have been.

What is North Dakota's largest natural lake? *See page 6 for the answer.*

How many buffalo roamed North America in the 1800s? *Page 10 has the answer.*

What does the name *Triceratops* mean? *See page 13 for the answer.*

Who was North Dakota's largest Native American group when settlers first arrived? *Turn to page 14 for the answer.*

When was Dakota Territory created? *Look on page 21 for the answer.*

What is North Dakota's capitol often called? *Look on page 33 for the answer.*

How many flowers grow in the International Peace Garden? *Turn to page 34 for the answer.*

CANADA

MINNESOTA

Dunseith

Minot

Devils Lake

Grand Forks

Missouri River

Watford City

Lake Sakakawea

Riverdale

Washburn

NORTH DAKOTA

Carrington

MONTANA

Badlands

Beulah

Bismarck

94

Jamestown

West Fargo

Red River

Fargo

Medora

Dickinson

Fort Ransom

29

SOUTH DAKOTA

STATE SYMBOLS

State beverage: Milk

State bird: Western meadowlark

State dance: Square dance

State fish: Northern pike

State flower: Wild prairie rose

State fossil: Teredo petrified wood

State grass: Western wheatgrass

State honorary equine: Nokota horse

State march: "Flickertail March"

State tree: American elm

State seal

STATE SONG

"NORTH DAKOTA HYMN"
Words by James W. Foley Jr., music by Dr. C. S. Putnam

North Dakota, North Dakota,
With thy prairies wide and free,
All thy sons and daughters love
  thee,
Fairest state from sea to sea;
North Dakota, North Dakota,
Here we pledge ourselves to
  thee.

Hear thy loyal children singing,
Songs of happiness and praise,
Far and long the echoes ringing,
Through the vastness of thy ways;
North Dakota, North Dakota,
We will serve thee all our days.

Onward, onward, onward going,
Light of courage in thine eyes,
Sweet the winds above thee
  blowing,
Green thy fields and fair thy skies.
North Dakota, North Dakota,
Brave the soul that in thee lies.

God of freedom, all victorious,
Give us Souls serene and strong,
Strength to make the future
  glorious,
Keep the echo of our song;
North Dakota, North Dakota,
In our hearts forever long.

That was a great trip! We have traveled all over North Dakota. There are a few places that we didn't have time for, though. Next time, we plan to visit the Children's Museum at Yunker Farm in Fargo. Kids can see the inside of a beehive, play with puppets, and study the stars! If there's time, visitors can even ride the carousel!

State flag

FAMOUS PEOPLE

Christopher, Warren (1925–), former U.S. secretary of state

Davies, Ronald N. (1904–1996), judge

Dickinson, Angie (1931–), actor

Dmitri, Ivan (1900–1968), artist

Duhamel, Josh (1973–), actor

Eielson, Carl Ben (1897–1929), pilot

Erdrich, Louise (1954–), novelist

Flannagan, John (1895–1942), sculptor

Gass, William H. (1924–), philosopher and novelist

Jackson, Phil (1945–), former basketball coach

L'Amour, Louis (1908–1988), novelist

Lee, Peggy (1920–2002), singer

Maris, Roger (1934–1985), baseball player

Oimoen, Casper (1906–1995), skier

Purpur, Cliff "Fido" (1912–2001), hockey player

Roosevelt, Theodore (1858–1919), 26th U.S. president

Rosenquist, James (1933–), painter

Sitting Bull (ca. 1831–1890), Lakota leader

Welk, Lawrence (1903–1992), television host

Woiwode, Larry (1941–), novelist

WORDS TO KNOW

bonanza farms (buh-NAN-zuh FARMZ) large and profitable farms

environment (en-VYE-run-muhnt) natural surroundings such as air, water, and soil

immigrants (IM-uh-gruhnts) people who move to another country

industry (IN-duh-stree) a type of business

international (in-tur-NASH-uh-nuhl) relating to two or more nations

pioneers (pye-uh-NEERZ) the first people who settle in an unsettled land

traditional (truh-DISH-uh-nul) following long-held customs

troll (TROLE) a creature in Scandinavian folklore that lives in caves or hills

TO LEARN MORE

IN THE LIBRARY

Nelson, S. D. *Sitting Bull: Lakota Warrior and Defender of His People*. New York, NY: Abrams Books, 2015.

Perritano, John. *The Lewis and Clark Expedition*. New York, NY: Scholastic, 2010.

Rosenstock, Barb. *The Camping Trip That Changed America: Theodore Roosevelt, John Muir, and Our National Parks*. New York, NY: Penguin Random House, 2012.

ON THE WEB

Visit our Web site for links about North Dakota:

childsworld.com/links

Note to Parents, Teachers, and Librarians: We routinely verify our Web links to make sure they are safe and active sites. So encourage your readers to check them out!

PLACES TO VISIT OR CONTACT

North Dakota Tourism Division

ndtourism.com
1600 East Century Avenue, Suite 2
Bismarck, ND 58502
800/435-5663
For more information about traveling in North Dakota

State Historical Society of North Dakota

history.nd.gov
612 East Boulevard Avenue
Bismarck, ND 58505
701/328-2666
For more information about the history of North Dakota

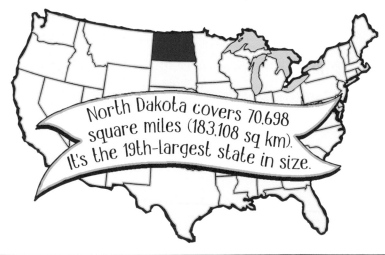

North Dakota covers 70,698 square miles (183,108 sq km). It's the 19th-largest state in size.

INDEX

Bye, Peace Garden State. We had a great time. We'll be back soon!